Looking Back

SHIPS IN TROUBLE
THE GREAT LAKES
1880 - 1950

Looking Back

SHIPS IN TROUBLE
THE GREAT LAKES
1880 - 1950

Skip Gillham

Looking Back Press

Copyright © by Skip Gillham. All rights reserved. No part of this book may be reproduced, stored in a retrieval system, or transmitted in any form without written permission of the publisher.

Vanwell Publishing acknowledges the financial support of the Government of Canada through the Book Publishing Industry Development Program for our publishing activities.

Published by Looking Back Press
An Imprint of Vanwell Publishing Limited
1 Northrup Crescent, P.O. Box 2131
St. Catharines, ON L2R 7S2
For all general information contact Looking Back Press at:
Telephone 905-937-3100 ext. 835
Fax 905-937-1760
E-Mail vanessa.kooter@vanwell.com

For customer service and orders:
Toll-free 1-800-661-6136

Printed in Canada

National Library of Canada Cataloguing in Publication

Gillham, Skip, 1941-
Ships in trouble : the Great Lakes, 1880-1950 / Skip Gillham.

(Looking back)
ISBN 1-55068-938-X

1. Shipwrecks—Great Lakes—History.   2. Ships—Great Lakes—Pictorial works.
I. Title.   II. Series: Looking back (St. Catharines, Ont.)

G525.G55 2005   971.3
C2005-902798-3

Lambton was battered by a storm on December 8, 1927, but survived for use as a barge. (Milwaukee Public Library)

Contents

Acknowledgements	6
Preface	7
Introduction	8
1. 1880 - 1920	9
2. 1921 - 1930	35
3. 1931 - 1940	61
4. 1941 - 1950	87

Acknowledgements

Collecting the information and gathering the photographs that appear in this volume has been an enjoyable hobby for over forty years. I am grateful to many organizations and individuals who have assisted in this task. Many of the illustrations have come from several outstanding collections. I am particularly grateful to Suzette Lopez of the Milwaukee Public Library for the support and opportunity to make others aware of their historical treasures by using some of their fine images.

Other valuable resources have been the collections of the Marine Historical Society of Detroit, the Canal Park Museum through their now retired Curator C. Patrick Labadie, the James Studio of Owen Sound, Great Lakes Graphics and Dave Wiley, Skyfotos from Great Britain, the World Ship Society, the St. Catharines Standard, the Marine Museum of the Great Lakes at Kingston as well as several individual collections. Thanks is extended to Louise Lowes for access to the fine collection of the late Captain Ken Lowes, the family of the late Alfred King, Jay Bascom for the use of the photos of John H. Bascom, the late George Ayoub for the use of the photos from the collection of Earl D. Simzer, Arden Phair of the St. Catharines Museum, Tracy Marsh of the Collingwood Museum, Trash and Treasures Barn of Ashtabula, Ohio, plus Barry Andersen, Jim Bartke, Ron Beaupre, Don Boone, Roger Chapman, Gordon Compton, George Corbin, Dave Glick, Hubert Hall of Shipsearch Marine, Doug Mackie, Ken Macpherson, Al Mann, Daniel C. McCormick, Gareth McNabb, Scott McWilliam, Ralph K. Roberts, Alfred Sagon-King, Albert Schelling, Craig Workman as well as friends who have passed away including Duff Brace, Bill Bruce, Rev. Edward J. Dowling, Alex Duncan, Doug Garrett, Ted Jones, Jim Kidd, Ernie Longman, R.T. McCannell, Paul Michaels, Clyde Sandelin, Paul Sherlock, Ken Smith, Al Sykes and Peter Worden.

Preface

Ships In Trouble 1880 – 1950 is the second book on the subject of marine accidents involving ships that worked on the Great Lakes. It follows *Ships In Trouble 1851 – 1930*, which was published in 2003. Each provides a chronological list of stories involving the troubles—some small, others significant—of a few of the ships that ply the inland seas.

Some of these vessels have been part of the author's many articles about shipwrecks that have appeared in the past in the *Dunnville Chronicle, Thorold News, Port Colborne News,* and *Jefferson Gazette.* They continue to run in the *Collingwood Enterprise-Bulletin, Goderich Signal Star, Niagara News, Port Colborne Leader, Weekend Edition of the Lincoln Post-Express, The Lightship* of the Lake Huron Lore Society, *Mariner's Weather Log* and *Going Places.* In addition his stories about the ships of the Great Lakes are weekly features in the *St. Catharines Standard, Port Huron Times Herald* and the *Sarnia Observer* as well as a variety of historic and corporate journals.

Introduction

The inland seas have a long legacy of shipwrecks. Lasalle's *Griffon*, the first sailing schooner on the upper lakes, disappeared on the initial voyage in 1679. *Walk-in-the-Water*, the first steamboat, was a casualty in 1821. *Eastland* is recognized as having the heaviest loss, claiming 835 lives when it rolled over and sank in the Chicago River on July 24, 1915.

The Great Lakes and their connecting channels can appear calm and enjoyable waterways for pleasure craft—but they can also bring death and destruction to the largest freighters. Each lake has its own stories of the famous "gales of November" bringing an end to lives, vessels and cargo with little or no warning. Some ships have gone down without a trace, others plunged to the depths in full view of onlookers who were unable to help.

The Great Storm of November 1913 claimed an estimated 250 lives, with Lake Huron bearing the brunt of the violent weather. The Armistice Day Storm of November 11, 1940, created havoc on Lake Michigan and three ships were lost. Sport divers continue to search for the final resting places of some of the giant steel freighters that perished.

Lake Erie, the shallowest of the five Great Lakes, most quickly builds ferocious waves which have caught many a mariner by surprise. Black Friday was the name given to October 20, 1916, a day on which four ships and over forty lives were lost.

Lake Ontario may have had the fewest casualties overall, but it is not immune to trouble. The worst disaster on that lake was the fiery demise of the beautiful passenger liner *Noronic* at Toronto on September 17, 1949, in which 118 lives were lost.

Some Great Lakes ships have left the inland seas for saltwater service. Many have successfully aided war efforts and helped to restore peace. Some of these became victims of enemy action, while others succumbed to storms, fires and groundings. In addition a few of the many deep sea visitors to the inland lakes have been lost back on their saltwater routes.

This book takes a look at some of the ships that have encountered trouble in their travels on the Great Lakes and abroad.

One
1880 - 1920

Lansdowne was built at Wyandotte, Michigan, in 1884 and began hauling railway cars across the Detroit River. The 294-foot-long sidewheel ferry had two tracks and a capacity for 14 cars. Navigating the busy waterway was a challenge [and a collision with Lansdowne sank the *Clarion* on July 15, 1884]. *Lansdowne* was retired in the 1980s and has seen sporadic service as a restaurant. (Dave Glick Collection)

The wooden passenger ferry *William Armstrong* was launched at Ogdensburg, New York, on November 23, 1876 and was rebuilt as a rail car ferry in 1882 for service across the St. Lawrence. The ship was swamped and sunk on June 30, 1889. One life was lost. The vessel was refloated, repaired and operated as the barge *Mons Meg* from 1910 to 1938 before it was abandoned. (L. Bovard, courtesy Dan McCormick)

Rothesay originally sailed on the St. John River in New Brunswick. It was built there in 1867 and came to the Great Lakes ten years later for service between Montreal and ports on Lake Ontario. The 193-foot-long passenger steamer collided with a tug near Prescott on September 12, 1889. Initially it was beached, and all on board *Rothesay* were saved but the ship later sank and was abandoned. (Dan McCormick Collection)

Nipigon was a wooden freighter built at St. Clair, Michigan, in 1883. The 194-foot-long ship hit the ore carrier *Vienna* broadside in fog on Whitefish Bay, Lake Superior, on September 16, 1892, and the *Vienna* went to the bottom. *Nipigon* was repaired and became *Maplehill* in 1920 and then *Maplegrange* later the same year. It was abandoned at Kingston in 1925 and scuttled in Lake Ontario during 1927. (Author's Collection)

Cibola was launched at Deseronto, Ontario, on November 1, 1887 and began service the following June, operating between Toronto and the Niagara River port of Lewiston. The 260-foot-long passenger steamer caught fire at Lewiston on July 15, 1895 and the Third Engineer perished. The burned-out hull was towed back to Toronto where the engine was salvaged for the *Corona* and the *Cibola*'s remains were used in a harbour landfill project. (Courtesy John H. Bascom)

Victory was the first 400-foot-long laker to be built. It was completed at Chicago in 1895. The ship loaded a record 160,000 bushels of barley at Duluth on November 25, 1895. It ran aground on Lansing Shoal on October 20, 1898 and arrived at Mackinaw City in leaking condition. The vessel was repaired and later survived the blizzard of 1905 and a grounding in the Great Storm of November 1913. (Marine Historical Society of Detroit)

Victory came to Canadian registry as *Victorious* in 1940. It had been lengthened to 472 feet in 1905 and spent the final years in the grain trade serving customers of Upper Lakes Shipping. It was retired after the 1968 season and then was sunk as a breakwall off the Canadian National Exhibition at Toronto during 1969. (SG)

Arthur Orr dated from 1893. The vessel stranded off Isle Royale, Lake Superior, on November 22, 1898. It was carrying 2,200 tons of flour, 500 tons of copper and a deckload of shingles at the time. The ship was refloated and lengthened to 334 feet in 1899. It served in a variety of trades until it was scrapped at Hamilton in 1947-48. (Great Lakes Graphics)

Aurora was launched at Cleveland on August 23, 1887, and joined the Corrigan fleet. The 290-foot-long wooden freighter became stuck in the ice of the Detroit River and caught fire on December 12, 1898. After salvage, the remains were rebuilt as a barge and survived until it was abandoned because of old age in 1927. (Marine Historical Society of Detroit)

Lakeside, launched at Windsor on April 10, 1888, usually operated across Lake Ontario between Port Dalhousie and Toronto. The 121-foot-long vessel sank at Port Dalhousie during fit out on March 24, 1905. Water was sucked in through a seacock after the engine that was filling the boiler shut down. *Lakeside* was refloated and operated until 1911. Rebuilt as the tug *Joseph L. Russell*, it sank in Lake Ontario on November 15, 1929. (Ken Lowes Collection)

After only fifteen years of service, the 261-foot-long wooden freighter *Hesper* was blown aground in 60 mile-per-hour winds near Silver Bay, Minnesota, on May 3-4, 1905. The ship was travelling in ballast for Two Harbors but struck a reef. All on board were rescued but the vessel was pounded to pieces. (Marine Historical Society of Detroit)

Venezuela was a wooden steamer dating from 1897. The 270-foot-long vessel was towing the schooner *Pretoria* when the schooner went aground in a storm off Outer Island, Lake Superior, on September 2, 1905. Five crew on board the barge were rescued but five more were lost. *Venezuela* became the barge *Erie* in 1923 and operated in the coal trade until it was abandoned at Sandusky in 1929. (Marine Historical Society of Detroit)

The *George Stephenson*, built in 1896, was 432 feet long and once held a Great Lakes record for carrying 323, 250 bushels of oats. The vessel was blown aground at Point aux Pins, Lake Superior, on September 3, 1905 and then was struck by her barge the *John A. Roebling*. Both ships were refloated and the *George Stephenson* survived until it was scrapped at Hamilton in 1963-64. (Paul Michaels Collection)

The 900-passenger steamer *Mayflower* was launched at Toronto on May 24, 1890. The 140-foot, 2-inch ferry cost $33,000, and connected Toronto and the Toronto Island communities. The ship was tied next to the ill-fated *Shamrock* which was destroyed by a fire on August 6, 1907. Alert crewmen had the *Turbinia* pull *Mayflower* from danger with only a small blaze on deck. The ship survived until retirement on August 30, 1938 and then worked as the barge *R.C.C. 26*. (John H. Bascom)

Edmonton, loaded with 35,000 bushels of grain, was downbound near the Brockville Narrows on September 6, 1907, when it hit a rock. The ship took on water and settled on the bottom. After it was pumped out, the 256-foot-long freighter was repaired at Kingston. Only a year old at the time, *Edmonton* sailed on for another 50 years and, after a brief retirement, was scrapped at Lauzon, Quebec, in 1961. (Earl D. Simzer Collection, courtesy of the late George Ayoub)

Alex Nimick was built at West Bay City, Michigan, and launched on January 25, 1890. The 320-foot-long wooden freighter was loaded with coal when it stranded on September 21, 1907. The vessel was en route from Buffalo to Duluth but hit bottom off Vermilion Point, Whitefish Bay on Lake Superior and broke up as a total loss. Six sailors perished in the accident. (Marine Historical Society of Detroit)

City of Grand Rapids dated from 1879 and was completed at Grand Haven, Michigan. The 138-foot-long passenger and freight steamer usually operated on Lake Michigan but came to Georgian Bay in 1907 for service out of Owen Sound, Ontario. The vessel did not last long as it caught fire at Tobermory, Ontario, on October 29, 1907. The blazing steamer was cut loose from the dock and allowed to drift into the bay where it burned and sank. (James Studio)

William E. Reis settled in 26 feet of water in the St. Clair River after a November 1, 1907, collision with the *Monroe C. Smith*. Salvage proved to be a challenge but finally succeeded on December 7 and repairs were reported to cost $100,000. The 436-foot-long bulk carrier became *Uranus* in 1916 and *Saskadoc* in 1926. It was scrapped at Santander, Spain, at the age of 68 after arriving under tow on September 24, 1967. (Marine Historical Society of Detroit)

Monroe C. Smith received bow damage in the November 1, 1907, collision with the *William E. Reis* and had to be beached at Russell Island. The 400-foot freighter was also repaired and it operated for the Great Lakes Steamship Company until the end of the Second World War. The ship is shown under tow for scrapping at Hamilton in 1947. (Ted Jones, courtesy Barry Andersen)

Pascal P. Pratt was built at Cleveland and launched on April 18, 1888. The 286-foot-long wooden steamer was travelling from Buffalo to Milwaukee with anthracite coal when it caught fire on November 16, 1908. The blaze began in the engine room and spread quickly. The Captain was able to beach the ship near Long Point, Lake Erie, and all on board were saved. (Milwaukee Public Library)

Canada was originally called the *J. W. Steinhoff* when it was built at Wallaceburg in 1874. The 130-foot, 4-inch passenger and freight carrier was renamed *Queen City* in 1895 and *Canada* in 1898. The ship was rebuilt in 1901 and sailed out of Owen Sound until destroyed by a fire about 1909. The remains of the hull were scuttled in Colpoy Bay, north of Owen Sound, about 1911. (James Studio)

City of Green Bay dated from 1880, when it was built as the *M.C. Howley* at Fort Howard, Wisconsin. The ship was renamed in 1887 and rebuilt for the lumber trade in 1908. The 140-foot-long freighter caught fire on Saginaw Bay, apparently caused by an exploding lantern, on August 19, 1909. The vessel was a total loss but all on board were picked up and brought to safety. (Rev. E. J. Dowling Collection)

Alexander Holley, a 376-foot-long whaleback barge, was being towed by the *Sir William Fairbairn*, when the towline broke in a storm on September 17, 1909. The powerless vessel wallowed out of control on Lake Superior until the anchors it had put down finally held just before the ship could strike the dangerous Eagle River Reef. It took five hours to rescue the crew. The ship survived until it was scrapped at Hamilton in 1965. (Capt. Ken Lowes Collection)

Ottawa was built at Toronto in 1900 and usually operated between the Lakehead and Depot Harbor on Georgian Bay. The 253-foot-long vessel left Port Arthur with wheat on November 14, 1909 and foundered the next day off Passage Island, Lake Superior, when the cargo shifted. The vessel sank stern first and the crew of eighteen managed to row the lifeboat through wild seas some fifty miles to the safety of Keweenaw Point. (Ron Beaupre Collection)

Badger State was built for the passenger and freight trade in 1862. The ship, rebuilt as a lumber carrier in 1905, was lost in 1909. The 213-foot-long freighter caught fire at Marine City, Michigan, on December 6, 1909 and drifted down the St. Clair River until it ran aground off Fawn Island. The hull burned to the waterline and was left to rot. (Milwaukee Public Library)

Geronia was launched at Collingwood on June 7, 1911 and went to work between Toronto and Quebec City. The 230-foot-long passenger carrier lost its propeller on the first trip back through the Cornwall Canal and later, on August 12, 1911, collided with the *H.P. Bigelow* near Brockville. The ship was also gashed running the Lachine Rapids on July 15, 1912. The vessel became the *Syracuse* in 1914, *Cape Trinity* in 1920 and was scrapped in 1937. (Ron Beaupre Collection)

Rensellaer had two collisions in 1912. The first on June 4, 1912 was with the *William H. Gratwick* on Lake Erie. Then, on August 7, 1912 it sank the *James Gayley* in foggy Lake Superior. The 474-foot-long *Rensellaer* sustained bow damage but was repaired and able to serve until the end of the Second World War. The ship was scrapped at Hamilton in 1947. (R.T. McCannell)

Marengo left Erie, Pennsylvania, under tow of the *Lloyd S. Porter* on October 12, 1912. The towline broke in rough weather and the 59.59-metre-long barge came ashore west of Port Colborne at Morgan's Point. The 34-year-old *Marengo* broke up but all on board were spared. The wreckage and cargo of coal were scattered on the bottom of the lake. (Don Boone Collection)

Juno was built at Wallaceburg in 1885 and rebuilt there in 1895. The 146-foot, 8-inch vessel lost a barge in a Lake Ontario storm on November 11, 1912 and arrived at Cobourg the next day, only to sink at the dock. Resold, *Juno* was salvaged but saw little, if any, service before it was sunk as a breakwall. (Ron Beaupre Collection)

Manitou carried fish, general freight and passengers between Goderich and the Canadian Lakehead communities of Fort William and Port Arthur. The 140-foot vessel was at Owen Sound for the winter when it caught fire and sank at the dock on February 2, 1913. Following repairs, it resumed service and survived a serious grounding on St. Joseph Island in the 1930s. *Manitou* was retired in 1939 and scrapped at Sorel, Quebec, in 1944. (James Studio)

Uganda was launched at West Bay City, Michigan, on, April 12, 1892 and worked in the coal and grain trades. The 310-foot-long freighter survived a grounding in Whitefish Bay on September 19, 1898. The hull was cut by the ice in the Straits of Mackinac and the ship sank near White Shoal, Lake Michigan, on April 19, 1913. No lives were lost. (Milwaukee Public Library)

Turret Chief was built at Sunderland, England, in 1896 and came to the Great Lakes in 1902. The 258-foot-long ship stranded east of Copper Harbor, Lake Superior, on November 8, 1913. The crew was found by Native Americans and saved. The ship was refloated using hydraulic jacks on July 6, 1914 and repaired. (World Ship Society)

City of Ottawa was originally the package freight and passenger carrier *India*. The vessel was built at Buffalo in 1871 and moved to Canadian registry as *City of Ottawa* in 1906. While upbound in the Cornwall Canal on May 13, 1914 it sheered to port and struck the downbound *S.N. Parent* at #2 hatch. The *City of Ottawa* survived until it was scrapped at Lake Pontchartrain, Louisiana, about 1945. (Earl D. Simzer Collection, courtesy of George Ayoub)

Paliki, originally Greek owned, was built at Sunderland, England, in 1889. It came to Canada for the Algoma Central Railway fleet in 1900. The 249-foot, 3-inch steamer was carrying steel rails for Chicago when it ran aground on Simmons Reef, near the Straits of Mackinac on April 19, 1915. The vessel later returned to saltwater and was scrapped in 1930 as the Italian freighter *Carmela*. (Gordon Crompton)

Collingwood was involved in a number of incidents between its construction at Collingwood in 1908 and its scrapping at Santander, Spain, in 1968. The 406-foot-long freighter stranded at Corsica Shoal, Lake Huron, on April 27, 1915 while downbound with grain and again in Whitefish Bay on April 23, 1916. Fire, collisions, a heroic rescue and even record cargos are also noted during this ship's very interesting career. (Capt. Ken Lowes Collection)

Eastland was launched at Port Huron, Michigan, on May 6, 1903 and soon began work in the passenger and fruit transportation trade on Lake Michigan. The 265-foot-long steamer was chartered to Western Electric for a company picnic trip to Michigan City, Indiana, when it rolled over at Chicago on July 24, 1915. The loss of 835 lives is the most in Great Lakes history and the cause of the tragedy was never clearly established. (Milwaukee Public Library)

Garden City was a popular passenger and freight carrier for the Niagara, St. Catharines and Toronto Navigation Company. The ship was built at Toronto in 1892 and ran into a severe storm crossing Lake Ontario on August 3, 1915. Windows were smashed by the waves and a hole was punched in the ship's side forcing it to turn back. Another steamer, the *Alexandria*, was lost. *Garden City* later worked at Montreal and was scrapped at Sorel in 1936-37. (St. Catharines Museum)

Henry Pedwell was built as the tug *Charles Lemcke* at Lions Head, Ontario, in 1909. It was renamed *Henry Pedwell* in 1913 and burned at the Wiarton dock on August 19, 1915. The 92-foot-long ship was salvaged, rebuilt and saw a variety of service on Georgian Bay as *Henry Pedwell*, *Kagawong* and then *Eastnor* before another fire at Wiarton claimed it on November 18, 1933. (Roger Chapman)

Midland Queen joined the Midland Navigation Company following construction at Dundee, Scotland, in 1901. It survived two collisions and two groundings before it was requisitioned for war service in 1915. The ship loaded war materials at Sydney, Nova Scotia, on July 21, 1915. It was sunk by gunfire from *U 28* near Fastnet, England, on August 4, 1915. The enemy submarine surfaced and warned the crew to abandon ship before they opened fire and sank it. (Capt. Ken Lowes Collection)

The first *Donnacona* served on the Great Lakes from 1900 until about 1915. It was built at Newcastle, England, in 1900 and operated in several Canadian fleets before returning to saltwater in the First World War. The ship was buffeted by a series of Atlantic storms and the hull finally cracked some 750 miles from the Azores on October 16, 1915. The 255-foot ore laden freighter sank but the crew was rescued. (Milwaukee Public Library)

Rock Ferry was built as the *Merrimac* at Wyandotte, Michigan, in 1882. The 251-foot-long wooden freighter was renamed *Rock Ferry* in 1911 and came to Canadian owners. The ship ran aground in fog off Main Duck Island, Lake Ontario, on May 17, 1916 but was salvaged and repaired. *Rock Ferry* later sailed in the Hall fleet before it was abandoned at Ogdensburg, New York, in 1924. (Willis Metcalfe, courtesy Dan McCormick)

Eastern States was a popular sidewheel passenger steamer that ran between Detroit and Buffalo. The 362-foot-long vessel was launched at Wyandotte, Michigan, on December 7, 1901, and sank the *Natironco* after a collision in the Detroit River on June 19, 1917. *Eastern States* later provided express service to Mackinac Island. The superstructure was deliberately burned off on December 12, 1956 and the hull was towed to Hamilton for scrapping, arriving on May 6, 1957. (Marine Historical Society of Detroit)

Home Smith was built as the *William S. Mack* in 1901 and operated under American registry before it was hit by the *Manitoba* in the fog of Whitefish Bay on July 9, 1917. The vessel was holed and intentionally beached to keep it from sinking. After repairs, the ship became *Home Smith* and then, in 1936, the *Algorail*. The 366-foot-long bulk carrier was scrapped at Toronto in 1963. (John H. Bascom)

Middlesex was built in 1880 as a steam powered lumber carrier but was rebuilt as a barge in 1882. The ship came to Canada for the Ontario Transportation and Pulp Company in 1916. The 184-foot-long vessel broke loose from a tug on August 13, 1917, and stranded at Rapide Plat in the St. Lawrence. *Middlesex* was initially abandoned but rebuilt in 1918 as the *Woodlands* and then scrapped in 1929. (Milwaukee Public Library)

The 73-foot-long *Island Queen* was built at Toronto in 1889 for the Island Park Ferry Company. The ship operated between downtown Toronto and the island communities of Hanlan's Point, Centre Island and Ward's Island. This ferry suffered fire damage in 1917 and was then destroyed by a blaze at Hanlan's Point on March 14, 1918 The remains were left to rot. (Jay Bascom)

The first *Impoco* was built for Imperial Oil in 1910 and came to the Great Lakes that fall. The 259-foot-long tanker returned to saltwater in 1913. Renamed *Waneta*, it was carrying fuel oil from Halifax to Ireland when sunk. A torpedo from *U 101* struck the vessel while south-southeast of Kinsale Head, Ireland, on May 30, 1918 and eight lives were lost. (Young photo, Jay Bascom Collection)

John F. Morrow, built in 1890, had previously sailed as the *John W. Moore* and *Edward N. Breitung*. Renamed in 1918, the 246-foot-long steamer was towing the *Santiago* when the barge began to leak while downbound on Lake Huron. The crew of the barge was rescued but their ship foundered off Pointe Aux Barques on September 10, 1918. *John F. Morrow* became *Kipawa* in 1927 and was scrapped at Sorel in 1944. (Ted Jones, courtesy Barry Andersen)

Doric was built at Toronto as the *Tadoussac* in 1903. The 260-foot-long vessel was renamed by Northern Navigation in 1907. *Doric* went overseas in 1916 and was damaged in a torpedo attack on May 1, 1917. Repaired and sold to French interests as *Buffalo*, the ship was sunk by *U 117* near Trevose Head, England, on September 18, 1918. (James Studio)

The 56-foot, 4-inch *Helen Taylor* worked around the lumber mill towns and often picked up logs or lumber that had escaped booms or washed overboard. Being short, wide and of shallow draft, this very stable vessel could go many places that were off limits to bigger ships. *Helen Taylor* was damaged during a fire in its pilot house near Hessel, Michigan, on October 7, 1919 but survived until it was scrapped about 1930. (Rev. E.J. Dowling Collection, courtesy Gareth McNabb)

A. McVittie had anything but a quiet career after the 253-foot, 4-inch steamer was built at Detroit in 1890. The ship was involved in a rescue in 1899, a collision in 1915 and stranded in 1918. It later took out a lock gate in the Welland Canal. *A. McVittie* was damaged in a storm in October 1919, sank at Kingston on November 21, 1919, and was scuttled in Lake Ontario in 1920. (Milwaukee Public Library)

Pawnee was built at Marine City, Michigan, and entered service on April 13, 1889, loading salt for Tobermory. The 180-foot-long freighter became *Maplegulf* in 1919 and broke its back in a Lake Ontario storm on November 5, 1920. The ship was beyond repair and was initially abandoned at Kingston. It was used again in 1925 and sunk as part of a Lake Erie salvage project. (Paul Michaels Collection)

Two
1921 - 1930

Russell Sage was originally a package freight carrier and operated by the Wabash Railroad between Toledo and Buffalo. The 230-foot-long vessel was rebuilt as a bulk carrier in 1897 and came to Canadian registry as the barge *Atlasco* in 1918. The ship caught fire and sank west of Kingston on August 7, 1921, while carrying a load of steel wire. All on board were saved and some of the cargo was later salvaged. (Milwaukee Public Library)

The first *Keywest* came from Wallsend, England, in 1909 and operated through the old canals. The 258-foot-long bulk carrier sank the schooner *Oliver Mowat* off the False Duck Islands, Lake Ontario, on September 21, 1921. Three lives were lost and the captain and mate were reportedly jailed for negligence. *Keywest* survived groundings in 1935 and 1938 but was broken up at Kingston in 1947 and the scrap shipped by rail to Algoma Steel at Sault Ste. Marie. (Earl D. Simzer Collection, courtesy George Ayoub)

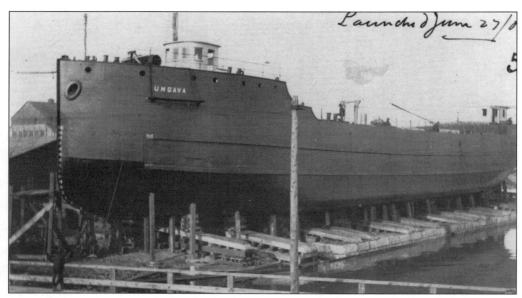

Ungava was a 206-foot-long barge. It was launched at Collingwood on June 27, 1906 and joined the Montreal Transportation Company for the grain run from Prescott to Montreal. It later hauled coal and grain for Canada Steamship Lines but went overseas in 1918. Renamed *Segre*, the ship sank at an undetermined location during November 1921. (Collingwood Museum)

Iron King joined the Detroit Transportation Company after it was built in 1887. The 268-foot-long wooden steamer came to the Lehigh Coal Company as *Canobie* in 1913. The vessel sustained considerable damage from a Lake Erie storm on November 1, 1921 and was leaking when it limped into port. The hull was stripped of valuable parts and the superstructure burned off. What remained was scuttled off Erie, Pennsylvania. (Capt. Ken Lowes)

Aragon dated from 1896 and was considered a total loss after stranding at Salmon Point, Lake Ontario, on November 7, 1921. The 256-foot-long steel steamer was refloated in 1922 and rebuilt. It became a self-unloading sandsucker in 1927 and then a regular self-unloader about 1942. The ship was renamed *Bayanna* in 1946 but suffered later groundings and a fire. (Roger Chapman)

Carmi A. Thompson was only four years old when driven ashore by gale force winds at Buffalo on December 18, 1921. The 550-foot-long steel steamship was then wedged between two other freighters and required the replacement of 156 hull plates after it was released on January 5, 1922. The vessel returned to service and became *Thorold* in 1963. The hull was broken up for scrap at Port Colborne in 1972. (Paul Michaels Collection)

Chief Wawatam was a powerful rail car ferry that connected the rail line across the Straits of Mackinac between Mackinaw City and St. Ignace, Michigan. The 351-foot-long steamer was usually a powerful icebreaker but was marooned for a week in 1922 and 160 passengers had to be evacuated by sleigh or on foot. The vessel tied up in August 1984 and was rebuilt as a barge in 1989-90. (Paul Michaels Collection)

Caribou was launched at Goderich on May 4, 1904 and was equipped to carry fish, freight and passengers between Owen Sound and Sault Ste. Marie, Ontario. The vessel ran aground in the Nelson Channel near Richards Landing on July 28, 1922 but was salvaged and operated through 1946. Plans to have the ship made into a tourist hotel at Sault Ste. Marie never materialized and the 150-foot-long vessel was eventually dismantled. (Ron Beaupre Collection)

Aube, originally *Rosemount*, was built for Great Lakes trading at Newcastle, England, in 1896. The ship returned to the Atlantic in the First World War before coming inland again in 1922. It ran aground in the St. Lawrence off Carleton Island, carrying 65,000 bushels of grain on September 25, 1922 and required extensive repairs at Kingston. The ship survived other escapades before it was broken up for scrap at Sorel, Quebec, in 1937-38. (John H. Bascom)

Glenmavis (left of *Glenlivet*), dated from 1913. The 256-foot, 5-inch bulk carrier collided with fleetmate *Glenclova* at Montreal on November 10, 1922 and suffered close to $10,000 in damage. The ship sailed for several owners before it became *Acadian* with Canada Steamship Lines in 1927. The hull was broken up at Kingston, Ontario, in 1959. (Capt. Ken Lowes)

Jos. W. Simpson was built at Wyandotte, Michigan, as *Manchester* in 1889, and scrapped at Sault Ste. Marie in 1960. It was renamed *Jos. W. Simpson* in 1921, *Mindemoya* in 1938 and *Yankcanuck* in 1946. The 256-foot, 9-inch vessel stranded near Tibbett's Point, Lake Ontario, while upbound from Ogdensburg, New York, to Milwaukee on November 12, 1922. The ship was released with close to $12,000 in damage and lasted for over seventy years. (Great Lakes Graphics)

Malton came to Canada in 1915 and had three collisions and a grounding before stranding at Main Duck Island, Lake Ontario, on November 17, 1922. The 260-foot-long freighter was stuck for almost two weeks. Once released, it was repaired at Kingston and survived until it was scrapped at Port Dalhousie in 1934. The vessel had been built in the United States as *E. M. Peck* in 1888. (Earl D. Simzer Collection, courtesy George Ayoub)

The 243-foot, 6-inch *Cadillac* was built at Chicago and launched on May 24, 1892. The ship sailed in the American ore trade for Cleveland-Cliffs but joined the Canadian Interlake Line in 1912. It became a charter member of the Canada Steamship Lines fleet in 1913 and was renamed *Maplehurst* in 1919. (Marine Historical Society of Detroit)

Maplehurst foundered on November 20, 1922. The ship was seeking shelter from a Lake Superior storm near the West Portage Entry when it lost power and the anchors failed to hold. The hull was driven aground and the superstructure washed away by the towering waves. Eleven lives were lost. (Paul Michaels Collection)

James P. Donaldson was built at Marine City, Michigan, in 1880 and originally sailed in the lumber trades. The 195-foot, 6-inch vessel joined N. M. Paterson and Sons Ltd. in 1920 and was used to bring wet grain to the storage elevator for drying. The *James P. Donaldson* caught fire at the Canadian Lakehead on March 18, 1923 and the remains were sunk off Isle Royale on May 6, 1923. (Paul Michaels Collection)

Brookdale was built as the wooden schooner *Moravia*. It was completed at West Bay City, Michigan, in 1888 and rebuilt as a barge in 1912. The name was changed to *Brookdale* in 1915 and it was used mainly in the grain trade for Canada Steamship Lines. The 222-foot-long vessel sank at Montreal on June 1, 1923 after a collision with the *Mapledawn*. The damage was significant and when *Brookdale* was refloated it was taken away and scrapped. (Bill Bruce Collection)

Nine survivors of the 37-year-old, 130-foot-long wooden steamer *W. J. Carter* were picked up by the *Keyport* when the *W. J. Carter* began leaking and foundered in Lake Ontario on July 28, 1923. *Keyport*, a 258-foot-long bulk carrier, had been built at Wallsend, England, in 1909 and was scrapped at Port Dalhousie, Ontario, in September 1963. (Ted Jones, courtesy Barry Andersen)

Harry R. Jones was built at Superior, Wisconsin, in 1903 and sailed as the *D.G. Kerr* until 1916. It sank the wooden steamer *Philetus Sawyer* in a collision off Windmill Point in the Detroit River on June 28, 1923. The 468-foot-long *Harry R. Jones* served the Interlake Steamship Company and Cargo Carriers Inc. before it was scrapped at Troon, Scotland, in 1961. (Author's Collection)

Luzon suffered serious damage when it ran aground northeast of Passage Island, Lake Superior, on October 17, 1923. The steamer, laden with grain, sustained damage to its bow and lost both anchors. Fortunately the forward bulkhead held, saving the ship but the Captain died of a stroke during the incident. The 366-foot-long freighter was rebuilt as the *John Anderson* (shown) in 1924 and was scrapped at Izmir, Turkey, as the *G.G. Post* in 1972. (Trash and Treasures Barn)

Linden was constructed at Port Huron, Michigan, and launched on December 15, 1894. It was built to carry copper ore from Lake Linden, Michigan, to Buffalo but later hauled lumber and pulpwood. The 215-foot-long steamer joined the Ontario Transportation and Pulp Company in 1918 but was again American owned when destroyed by a fire at Tawas Bay, Michigan on November 28, 1923. (Capt. Ken Lowes Collection)

The rail car ferry *Ontario No. 1* plied the waters of Lake Ontario between Cobourg and Rochester from 1907 to 1949. The 316-foot, 1-inch vessel cost $370,000 when built at Toronto and could make two round trips a day. After a rough passage on January 6-7, 1924, the ship arrived at Toronto with three feet of ice on deck. Without a stern seagate, the ferry had to head into the wind and could not enter the harbour at Cobourg. The vessel was scrapped at Port Colborne in 1951. (Ted Jones, courtesy Barry Andersen)

Brookton got lost in a spring snowstorm and stranded at Russell Island Shoal, near Owen Sound on April 22, 1924. The 256-foot-long bulk carrier was refloated the following day and the damage was repaired at the next regular drydocking. The ship had been built at Toronto in 1902 and had previously sailed as *Tadoussac, The Iroquois, Colorado* and *Dornoch* and later operated as *George Hindman* and the second *Brookdale* before it was scrapped at Hamilton in 1966-67. (Earl D. Simzer Collection, courtesy George Ayoub)

Ontario No. 2 was built at Toronto in 1915 and usually carried rail cars of coal across Lake Ontario. The ship added vehicles, as space permitted, in 1927. This ferry was approaching Cobourg in fog on August 6, 1924, missed the entry and was stranded on the beach until the next day. The 317-foot, 6-inch vessel survived a major fire at Cobourg on December 25, 1943, and was scrapped at Port Dalhousie and Hamilton in 1951-52. (Alfred King)

Mapleglen saw only limited service. The ship had been active as the *Wyoming* from 1887 until becoming *Mapleglen* in 1920. It often carried coal to Depot Harbour, Ontario, and was laid up by Canada Steamship Lines at Kingston in 1921. The vessel was deteriorating and had to be towed to a deep part of Lake Ontario near Amherst Island, on June 19, 1925, and scuttled. (Doug Garrett)

Pueblo came to Canada in 1913. It was renamed *Richard W.* in 1916 and *Palm Bay* in 1923. The 236-foot-long vessel was retired in 1925 and laid up at Portsmouth, Ontario. Fire struck on January 16, 1926, and the wooden hulled ship was destroyed. The remains were eventually scuttled in Lake Ontario in 1937. (Dan McCormick Collection)

John P. Reiss was backing from the National Harbours Board grain elevator at Port Colborne on May 9, 1926 when it struck the *A. D. MacBeth*. The 524-foot-long American bulk carrier was also damaged when it stranded at Ballard's Reef on November 10, 1930, and again when it hit the bank of the Black Rock Canal on May 15, 1933. This member of the Reiss Steamship Company fleet was built at Lorain, Ohio, in 1910 and scrapped at Castellon, Spain, in 1973. (Robert Walton)

New York News broke loose in a storm at Shelter Bay, Quebec, on October 26, 1926. With no radio contact on board, the ship was reported as lost until the weather cleared. The vessel had drifted away and gone aground on the rocky shore of the St. Lawrence. The 258-foot-long newsprint, pulpwood and grain carrier was eventually refloated and returned to service. (James Roberts)

New York News was renamed *Shelter Bay* in 1933 and worked for the Quebec and Ontario Transportation Company. The vessel continued in the regular bulk trades and often called at the company dock at Thorold, Ontario, to deliver pulpwood or load newsprint. During the Second World War, *Shelter Bay* saw some service on saltwater and was sold to N.M. Paterson and Sons Ltd. in 1958. (Ted Jones, courtesy Barry Andersen)

Shelter Bay was renamed *Labradoc* when it joined the Paterson fleet in 1958. The St. Lawrence Seaway was nearing completion, but the ship was acquired to carry grain from the Great Lakes to the St. Lawrence to fulfill company contracts until the giant canal project was opened to shipping. *Labradoc* was tied up at Kingston in the fall of 1959 and eventually sold for scrap. It arrived at Port Dalhousie in August 1961 and was soon broken up. (Peter Worden)

Casco operated for the Canada Starch Company and had two problems in 1927. The ship ran aground at Pipe Island in the Lower St. Mary's River on August 3 and had to be lightened to be released. Then on September 4 it went aground while leaving Cardinal, Ontario, and was again damaged. The 261-foot-long freighter was built at Hull, England, in 1927 and later operated as *Thordoc* and *Chembarge No. 2*. (Ted Jones, courtesy Barry Andersen)

Jolly Inez, noted earlier in trouble as *Turret Chief* (p. 25), stranded at Saddleback Island, False Detour Channel, on November 16, 1927 and had to be abandoned. There were problems with the insurers but the hull was eventually refloated and used as the stone barge *Salvor*. It broke loose of the tug *Richard Fitzgerald* on September 26, 1930 and sank off Muskegon, Michigan. (Earl D. Simzer Collection, courtesy George Ayoub)

Advance was built by Louis Shickluna at St. Catharines in 1884 and sailed as *Sir L.S. Tilley* until it was renamed in 1904. The 175-foot-long wooden steamer was used in the coal trade in the 1920s and ran aground off Manitoulin Island on December 5, 1927. The ship was badly damaged and, although salvaged, was laid up at Cornwall and stripped of useful parts before it was abandoned. (John H. Bascom)

Agawa, built as a barge in 1902 and powered in 1907, struck Advance Reef along the south shore of Manitoulin Island, on December 7, 1927. The vessel spent the winter aground and, after it was refloated on May 16, 1928, was towed to Collingwood and eventually repaired. The 390-foot-long bulk carrier returned to work in 1929 as *Robert P. Durham*. Later sales brought name changes to *Heron Bay* in 1940 and *Federal Husky* in 1963. The ship was towed to Bilbao, Spain and scrapped in 1965-66. (Milwaukee Public Library)

Lambton was built at Port Arthur, Ontario, as *Glenafton* in 1921 and was renamed when it joined the Mathews Steamship Company in 1925. The grain-laden vessel was downbound under terrible weather conditions when it stranded on Parisienne Shoal, Lake Superior, on December 28, 1927. Two sailors were lost but eighteen survived after rowing ashore. The hull was refloated and saw use as a barge until scrapped. (Milwaukee Public Library)

Huronic was Hull 1 at the Collingwood shipyard and it entered service on May 24, 1902. The 340-foot-long passenger and freight steamer ran aground at Lucille Island on August 6, 1928 and was high and dry for ten days. Salvage and repair costs topped $100,000 but the ship returned to service only to go aground again off Isle Royale in 1929. *Huronic* sailed for Canada Steamship Lines and was scrapped at Hamilton in 1950. (Doug Garrett Collection)

A Lake Huron storm drove the *W. H. Sawyer* to seek shelter on August 11, 1928. The salt-laden wooden freighter, with two barges in tow, almost made it but stranded off Harbor Beach Light, Lake Huron, about 100 yards from safety. The waves broke up the 215-foot-long steamer but only one life was lost. (Milwaukee Public Library)

Parks Foster dated from 1889 and originally worked as a package freight carrier. The vessel was shortened to 260 feet in 1921 and stranded in fog on Lake Huron near Alpena, Michigan, on October 16, 1928. The cargo was unloaded to barges and, after it was pumped out, the vessel was released and repaired. It returned to service as *Superior* in 1930 and was scrapped at Port Weller in 1961. (Earl D. Simzer Collection, courtesy George Ayoub)

Deepwater was built at Hull, England, in 1928 and came to Canada for Great Lakes service. This bulk carrier had loaded grain at Buffalo for Montreal when it got lost in fog on October 28, 1928. The 260-foot-long vessel was soon aground off Sugar Loaf Point, west of Port Colborne. It was released four days later. The ship became *Keymont* in 1939, *Hamildoc* in 1947 and was scrapped at Port Dalhousie in 1962. (James M. Kidd)

Owana provided passenger excursion service out of Detroit for the White Star Line. The ship was built as the *Pennsylvania* in 1899, renamed *Owana* in 1902 and then *Erie* in 1927. On February 2, 1929 during winter lay-up at Ecorse, Michigan, the vessel was destroyed by a fire. The hull was rebuilt as the coal barge *T. A. Ivey* in 1934 and operated on Lake Erie until 1963. Later renamed *Erie*, it was eventually sunk as a breakwall. (Marine Historical Society of Detroit)

Ralph Budd ran aground at Saltese Point on Lake Superior, near Eagle Harbor, Michigan, on May 15, 1929. The 402-foot, 6-inch vessel had just left Duluth with grain when it got into trouble. Although abandoned to the underwriters as a total loss, the vessel was salvaged and repaired. It later joined Upper Lakes and St. Lawrence Transportation and became *L. A. McCorquodale* in 1959 before it was scrapped at Hamilton in 1966. (Paul Michaels Collection)

John Hanlan was built by John Abbey at Port Dalhousie in 1884. The ship ran between Toronto and the Toronto Island community of Hanlan's Point with occasional trips across the western end of Lake Ontario to pick up fresh Niagara fruit. The vessel failed its inspection in 1929 and was torched as a spectacle off the Sunnyside Amusement Park at Toronto on June 19, 1929. (Roger Chapman)

The *Edward Buckley* was a fire victim on September 1, 1929. This 162-foot, 3-inch wooden freighter was en route to Little Current on Manitoulin Island to load pulpwood when a blaze broke out in the after end. The vessel burned to the waterline near Narrow Island Lighthouse on the North Channel of Georgian Bay and was a total loss. Area fishermen saved the crew. (Milwaukee Public Library)

Andaste was built at Cleveland in 1892 and originally worked in the iron ore trade. The ship was rebuilt as a self-unloading sand and gravel carrier in 1925. The loaded freighter was bound for Chicago when it got caught by a strong northwest gale in Lake Michigan on September 9-10, 1929. Somewhere out on the lake *Andaste* foundered and all twenty-five sailors on board were lost. (Marine Historical Society of Detroit)

The rail car ferry *Milwaukee* crossed Lake Michigan between Grand Haven and Milwaukee. The 358-foot-long vessel was swamped by heavy seas and disappeared with all hands off Racine, Wisconsin, on October 22, 1929. The loss of the 26-year-old ship resulted in a law being enacted to raise the height of the stern gate. The hull was found in 200 feet of water in 1963 and it sits upright on the bottom of the lake. (Capt. Ken Lowes Collection)

N. J. Nessen sank in April 1907 after it was punctured by ice. The ship was refloated and survived until it stranded on Lake Erie near Leamington, Ontario, on October 22, 1929. The ship was bound for Cleveland with a load of scrap steel and had been seeking shelter when it was left exposed by changing winds. The 156-foot, 9-inch freighter blew aground and the hull cracked and then broke up. All on board reached shore safely. (Milwaukee Public Library)

Wisconsin was built in 1881 and was renamed several times before becoming *Wisconsin* again in 1924. The 215-foot-long passenger and freight carrier survived a fire in 1907 and saltwater service during the First World War. The ship was sailing between Chicago and Milwaukee when it foundered off Kenosha, Wisconsin, on October 29, 1929. Sixteen lives were lost among the seventy-five passengers and crew. (Milwaukee Public Library)

The 33-year-old *Senator* was loaded with 241 new Nash automobiles when it sank on Lake Michigan. The accident occurred in heavy fog off Port Washington, Wisconsin, on October 31, 1929. The vessel was hit on the port side by the *Marquette* and went down in five minutes. Seven or eight sailors lost their lives while the survivors were picked up by the tug *Delos H. Smith*. (Milwaukee Public Library)

Briton sailed in several fleets from 1891 until it was wrecked on Lake Erie off Point Abino, Ontario, on November 13, 1929. A faulty fog signal was blamed for the 312-foot, 6 inch grain carrier going aground. The ship was battered for two days during salvage attempts but these efforts had to be abandoned. The remains of the vessel were dynamited after some of the grain had been removed. (James Studio)

Ulva was built in Scotland as *Caronpark* in 1912. The ship served on saltwater and became *Ulva* in 1922. The 241-foot freighter got caught in ice at Port Colborne on December 7, 1929 and sank. The vessel was refloated, repaired and returned to service in 1930. It continued to visit the Great Lakes in later years but was torpedoed and sunk northwest of Ireland on September 3, 1940. (Alfred King)

Claremont was built as *Erwin L. Fisher* and launched at Toledo on June 4, 1910. It sank following a collision the next year but was refloated and served on the Atlantic during the First World War. It came to Canadian registry as *Claremont* in 1923 and was lost shortly after becoming *George J. Whalen* in 1930. It had been rebuilt as a sandsucker and capsized in heavy seas off Dunkirk, New York, on July 29, 1930. Fifteen of the twenty-one on board were lost. (Earl D. Simzer Collection, courtesy George Ayoub)

Our Son was perhaps the last Great Lakes sailing vessel operating in the bulk trades. The ship dated from 1875 and was lost 40 miles west-southwest of Big Sable Point, Lake Michigan, on September 26, 1930. All on board the 190-foot-long schooner were picked up by the steel steamer *William Nelson* and saved. (Paul Michaels Collection)

Three
1931 - 1940

John J. Boland Jr. was built on speculation as *Tyneville* at Wallsend, England, in 1928 and then sold to the Sarnia Steamship Co. on completion. The 258-foot-long bulk carrier came to Canada, only to be lost on October 5, 1932. The vessel left Erie, Pennsylvania, with a load of coal for Hamilton but was soon flooded by heavy seas, rolled over and sank off Barcelona, New York. Four lives were lost. (Milwaukee Public Library)

Brown Beaver was tied up for the winter at Toronto when a fire broke out in the coal bunker on December 18, 1932. The Toronto Fire Department responded to the blaze and minimized the damage to the 259-foot-long grain-laden freighter. The vessel mainly worked for the Upper Lakes and St. Lawrence Transportation Company and had been built in England as *Fulton* in 1929. It was scrapped at Toronto in 1965. (Alfred King)

William Schupp ran aground off Cockburn Island, Lake Huron, on May 1, 1933. The 259-foot-long freighter was travelling without cargo from Goderich to Fort William when it stranded After it was refloated, the vessel was repaired at Collingwood for just over $24,000. The British built ship joined the N. M. Paterson and Sons fleet as *Mondoc* in 1945 and was scrapped at Deseronto, Ontario, in 1961. (Alfred King)

Brentwood was built at Collingwood as *W. D. Matthews* in 1903 and renamed by Canada Steamship Lines in 1926. The 375-foot-long bulk carrier ran aground in the St. Mary's River on June 15, 1933 and was released four days later. The ship tied up at Midland later in the year and was scrapped there in 1937. (Milwaukee Public Library)

George M. Cox was refitted in 1933 for passenger transport to the World's Fair at Chicago. The 237-foot-long passenger ship was built as *Puritan* in 1901 and was lost on a goodwill voyage on May 27, 1933. The vessel struck Rock of Ages Reef on Lake Superior in fog and hung at a precarious angle before sliding off into deep water in an October storm. All on board were rescued. (Milwaukee Public Library)

Sonora was delivered to the Superior Steamship Company on July 3, 1902. The 366-foot-long ship was en route from Buffalo to Chicago with sugar when it was in a collision with the *William Nelson* in the Bar Point Channel on July 17, 1933. Both vessels were determined to be equally at fault. In 1948 *Sonora* delivered a deckload of new Packard automobiles to Duluth for use as taxis. The ship was broken up at Ashtabula, Ohio, in 1961. (Marine Historical Society of Detroit)

D. E. Callendar was built at Cleveland as the *Yale* in 1895. The 380-foot-long bulk carrier was renamed *D. E. Callendar* in 1925 and stranded off Long Point, Lake Erie, on November 14, 1933. The vessel got lost in blinding snow and hit bottom at 0400 hours. The wheat-laden laker was refloated but never sailed again. It was apparently broken up at New Orleans during the Second World War. (Milwaukee Public Library)

Canadoc went hard aground at St. Joseph's Island in the St. Mary's River on May 8, 1934. The 436-foot-long bulk carrier had its steel hull punctured by a rock and water poured into the hold. This member of the Paterson fleet was later released and drydocked for repairs. The ship had been built at Cleveland as *H. C. Frick* in 1899 and was scrapped at Vado, Italy, as *Portadoc* in 1970. (Ted Jones, courtesy Barry Andersen)

Keybar stranded near Sault Ste. Marie, going aground on May 11, 1934. The damage to this 261-foot-long vessel was not too serious and it was pulled free after twelve hours on the bottom. *Keybar*, built at South Bank, England, in 1923, was used to carry grain, coal and pulpwood. It was scrapped at Port Dalhousie, Ontario, in the fall of 1963. (Dan McCormick)

Lyman M. Davis was built in 1873 and helped carry lumber to Chicago to meet reconstruction needs arising from the Great Fire at that city in 1871. The 123-foot-long wooden schooner later worked around Manitoulin Island and then in the Lake Ontario coal trade. Despite strong opposition, the *Lyman M. Davis* was torched as a spectacle off the Sunnyside Amusement Park at Toronto on June 29, 1934. (Milwaukee Public Library)

Saskadoc was almost lost on Lake Erie. The 436-foot-long vessel departed Erie, Pennsylvania, on September 27, 1934, with 7,500 tons of coal. The hatches were left open for the short run to the Welland Canal and this was almost a fatal mistake. The ship encountered wind and waves beyond their expectations and some of the coal was washed overboard. *Saskadoc* was listing when it arrived at Port Colborne eleven hours late, but all on board were safe. (SG)

The 33-year-old *William A. Reiss* stranded off the piers of Sheboygan, Wisconsin, while inbound with coal on November 13, 1934. The 450-foot-long steamer received considerable bottom damage and lost its rudder. The vessel was released, unloaded and discovered to be beyond economical repair. The ship was towed to Sturgeon Bay and broken up for scrap but the pilothouse was saved as a summer cottage. (Great Lakes Graphics)

Edward E. Loomis was a package freight carrier operating between Duluth, Chicago and Buffalo. The 404-foot-long vessel had been built as *Wilkesbarre* in 1901 and renamed in 1920. This ship sank the *W.C. Franz* in a collision on Lake Huron off Thunder Bay on November 21, 1934. The *Edward E. Loomis* rescued sixteen sailors but was severely damaged and never ran again. The hull was laid up at Buffalo and then towed to Hamilton in 1940 and broken up. (Milwaukee Public Library)

W.C. Franz sank following the November 21, 1934, collision with the *Edward E. Loomis*. The ship was hit on the port bow and sustained serious damage. The starboard lifeboat did not launch properly, tossing ten sailors into the lake. The *W.C. Franz* remained afloat for two hours before going down bow first. Four lives were lost from the crew of the 366-foot-long, 33-year-old ship. (Alan Mann)

Henry Cort was built as the *Pillsbury* in 1892 and had worked as a package freighter, ore carrier and craneship. The 335-foot-long whaleback steamer survived a collision, a grounding and two sinkings only to sail again. The ship was a total loss when it hit the north pier while seeking shelter at Muskegon, Michigan, on December 1, 1934. All on board were saved but a rescuer perished when a Coast Guard surfboat overturned. (Milwaukee Public Library)

A rare shipbuilding contract during the Great Depression led to the construction of the *Joseph Medill* at Wallsend, England. The 259-foot-long freighter was designed to carry newsprint and pulpwood and departed England for Montreal with 2,784 tons of anthracite coal on August 10, 1935. The ship was sighted a week later but was lost in the Atlantic with all hands. It is presumed the cargo shifted in a storm and the vessel rolled over. (George Corbin)

Hurry-On was a British cargo ship that came to the Great Lakes in 1934. The 11-year-old, 174-foot-long vessel was hit by a large wave after leaving the Strait of Canso on September 23, 1935 and began to list. When the list increased the crew abandoned ship off Port Hood Island, Nova Scotia. The lifeboat swamped twice and five of the twelve on board died of exposure before help arrived. (Shipsearch Marine)

Agga was a Norwegian owned freighter that came to the Great Lakes on several occasions. The 228-foot, 7-inch cargo carrier dated from 1905 and began inland voyages as early as 1923, visiting Toledo, Ohio, Chicago, Illinois, and South Haven, Michigan, over the years. The vessel was reported wrecked at Gunnorstenarne, Sweden, on December 29, 1935. (Deno Photo, courtesy Dan McCormick)

Aycliffe Hall was travelling upbound and lightship through dense fog near Long Point, Lake Erie, when there was a collision with the *Edward J. Berwind*. The June 11, 1936 accident ripped open the hull on the after end of the port side at about 0500 hours in the morning. The 258-foot, 6-inch Canadian freighter sank after all on board were saved. A salvage effort the next year almost succeeded but the ship slipped back to the bottom in a storm and was abandoned. (Earl D. Simzer Collection, courtesy George Ayoub)

Tashmoo was a popular passenger vessel from 1900 to 1936. The 308-foot-long ship had a justified reputation for speed. Its end came on June 18, 1936 when the hull was damaged by striking a submerged object in the Detroit River. *Tashmoo* reached the Amherstburg dock to unload its passengers but soon settled on the bottom. The keel snapped during salvage and the only choice was to scrap the remains. (Marine Historical Society of Detroit)

Chippewa was built at Hamilton in 1893 and could carry 2,000 passengers on the well travelled route between Toronto and Niagara River ports. The 320-foot-long vessel was battered by an August gale on Lake Ontario and the superstructure was shifted out of alignment. Repairs were too expensive to be made and the vessel was tied up at Toronto, stripped and towed to Hamilton and broken up in 1939. (Alfred King)

Benmaple was American and then French owned before coming to Canada for the Port Colborne and St. Lawrence Navigation Company in 1922. The ship was used in the grain trade until it was run down by the liner *Lafayette* and sunk in the St. Lawrence 200 miles below Quebec City. One sailor, who was crushed in his bunk, perished and the 22-year-old, 256-foot-long *Benmaple* sank in deep water on September 1, 1936. (Alfred King)

Sand Merchant was built in 1927 and rebuilt as a self-unloading sandsucker in 1930. The ship was caught in a Lake Erie storm on October 17, 1936 and took on water faster than the pumps could discharge it. The 259-foot-long vessel began to list and then rolled over. Only seven survived as the crew abandoned the ship before it sank. Nineteen were lost when their lifeboat overturned and the rest hung on until dawn when help arrived. (Great Lakes Graphics)

The passenger and freight carrier *Alice* was built at Toronto in 1907 and became *Hibou* in 1928. The vessel and seven crew were lost near Owen Sound on November 21, 1936 when the ship rolled over and sank. Ten reached shore safely. *Hibou* was not refloated until 1942 but was sold for saltwater service and rebuilt at Sorel, Quebec. The ship foundered off Tocopilla, Chile, on March 24, 1953. (Roger Chapman Collection)

Emperor had 9,000 tons of coal on board when one of the gales of November swept Lake Superior on November 25, 1936. The 525-foot-long bulk carrier, part of the Canada Steamship Lines fleet, lost its rudder and wallowed badly in the waves. One crewman was swept overboard but the crew of the *Renvoyle* was able to connect a towline to the *Emperor* and bring the disabled freighter to the safety of Port Arthur. (Al Sykes Collection)

Trenora left Sydney, Nova Scotia, on October 17, 1937 with a load of coal for Hamilton, when there was a build-up of coal gas in its hold. The subsequent explosion and fire at sea sent seven sailors to hospital with injuries. The ship's deck and bulkheads were bent and the forward cabin damaged. The 79.55-metre-long bulk carrier was rebuilt at Port Dalhousie, Ontario. It was renamed *Keyshey* in 1949 and scrapped at Bilbao, Spain, in 1967. (Ken Lowes Collection)

The 236-foot, 3-inch wooden bulk freighter *Sarnor* was laid up at Kingston near the LaSalle Causeway about 1923. It settled on the bottom and was heavily damaged by a serious fire on March 15, 1926. The hull was moved to nearby Portsmouth where it eventually sank. The remains were raised on November 1, 1937, towed into Lake Ontario and scuttled. (Author's Collection)

Waubic was built at Collingwood in 1909. The vessel was damaged by a fire while at winter quarters in Kingsville, Ontario, on January 18, 1938. The Lake Erie based 142-foot-long passenger steamer was towed to Port Dalhousie and rebuilt as the *Erie Isle*. Beginning in 1943, the ship operated to Prince Edward Island as *Prince Nova* but was destroyed by a fire at Pictou, Nova Scotia, on July 6, 1959. (Milwaukee Public Library)

City of Buffalo was fitting out for the 1938 season when a fire broke out on March 10. The cause was unknown but it resulted in an estimated $700,000 in damage. Eleven fire companies responded as flames shot 100 feet in the air. The 317-foot-long passenger vessel had been built in 1896 and was towed to River Rouge, Michigan, for scrapping in 1940. (Milwaukee Public Library)

The steering cable aboard *Redfern* broke in the Welland Canal at Dain City on June 24, 1938. The freighter, now out of control, hit the west bank and had to go to Port Colborne for repairs. Later, on July 7, 1938, further steering problems at Point Edward almost led to a collision with the *Huronic* and put *Redfern* aground. The ship survived until sinking in the Gulf of St. Lawrence as *Zenava* on April 28, 1971. (George Ayoub Collection)

Islet Prince was built as the tug *Mariposa* in 1902. It was rebuilt for passenger and freight service as *Bon Ami* in 1909 and became *Islet Prince* in 1926. The ship had stopped for the night near Southampton, Ontario on July 18, 1938 when it was hit by lightning. The 105-foot-long vessel caught fire and sank but all on board were saved. (James Studio)

The first *Windoc* was upbound in the Welland Canal on October 2, 1938 when Bridge 20 was lowered prematurely. The descending structure raked the deck toppling the stack, spar and lifeboats. The 430-foot-long steamer, a member of the N.M. Paterson fleet, was idle for eight days of repairs at Port Colborne. The ship had been built at Cleveland in 1899 and was broken up at La Spezia, Italy, in 1968. (Alfred Sagon-King)

Northton was built at Newcastle, England, and arrived at Toronto with a cargo of coal on July 25, 1924. The 261-foot-long vessel sank in Port Colborne harbour on February 2, 1939, after water leaked into the hull. The storage load of wheat expanded, heaving the hatch covers, but the ship was soon refloated and was taken to Port Dalhousie for repairs in the spring. It became *Novadoc* in 1946 and sank off Portland, Maine, during a storm on March 2, 1947. All on board perished. (Ted Jones, courtesy Barry Andersen)

Valley Camp was one of the earliest self-unloaders on the Canadian side of the Great Lakes. The 259-foot, 6-inch vessel was built at Newcastle, England, in 1927. The ship was proceeding in fog when it landed on Cole's Shoal near Brockville on April 19, 1939. *Valley Camp* was not released until April 24. The ship was lengthened in 1951, renamed *Valleydale* in 1965 and scrapped at Hamilton in 1967. (Alfred King)

Algosoo was headed for a north shore Georgian Bay port to load stone when it hit bottom near Cape Smith. The damage required immediate attention and the vessel arrived at Collingwood for repairs on July 1, 1939. The 366-foot-long bulk carrier dated from 1901 and was noted to have sailed over two million miles and carried over fourteen million tons of cargo for Algoma Central before it was scrapped at Bilbao, Spain, in 1967. (Paul Sherlock)

The 68-foot, 8-inch *R. P. Reidenbach* was towing the *E.A.S. Clarke* at Ashtabula, Ohio, on October 28, 1939 when the small tug rolled over and sank. Two men working below deck were lost and it is thought that the wash from the *E.A.S. Clarke's* propeller swamped the tug. The 29-year-old ship was refloated, repaired and worked as *Cornell* before it was scrapped at Ashtabula in 1964. (Duff Brace Collection)

Vardefjell was the first member of the Norwegian-flag Fjell Line to come to the Great Lakes when it arrived in 1932. The 246-foot, 6-inch freighter had been built for the North Sea coal trade and made several visits to the inland seas. It was sold to Lithuanian interests and renamed *Kaunas* in 1938. This vessel was an early casualty of the Second World War and was sunk by *U 57* on November 17, 1939. (Alfred King)

Thordoc stranded in fog on Cape Breton Island at Winging Point on March 30, 1940. The ship had gone east for coastal service after years of Great Lakes trading. The 259-foot-long vessel had been built at Newcastle, England, in1908 as *J. A. McKee* and joined the Paterson fleet as *Thordoc* in 1926. The twenty-one crewmembers safely reached shore but their ship was abandoned as a total loss. (C.F. McBride, courtesy Shipsearch Marine)

Arlington was on its second trip of the season when the wheat-laden steamer foundered on May 1, 1940. Water entered two hatches and the bulkhead gave way as a result of the swelling grain. The incoming water also flooded the engine room. The 257-foot-long, 27-year-old bulk carrier sank stern first into the cold waters of Lake Superior and the Captain was lost with his ship. (Earl D. Simzer Collection, courtesy George Ayoub)

Acadialite was sailing for Imperial Oil when it stranded at Cape Hurd, Bruce Peninsula, on June 30, 1940. The vessel cut too close to shore and required a trip to the Collingwood shipyard and $100,000 in repairs. The 256-foot, 3-inch tanker was renamed *Imperial Cornwall* in 1947 and *Golden Sable* in 1971. It was laid up later that year and eventually scrapped at Louiseville, Quebec, about 1980. (Earl D. Simzer Collection, courtesy George Ayoub)

Magog of Canada Steamship Lines was the first Canadian merchant ship sunk by enemy action in the Second World War. The 259-foot-long steamship was hit by a torpedo from *U 99* and was then sunk by gunfire on July 5, 1940. The U-boat commander gave the crew a bottle of brandy to share during their time in the lifeboat and all were picked up by a Finnish freighter and landed safely in Scotland. (Earl D. Simzer Collection, courtesy George Ayoub)

At low tide *Lachinedoc* was fully aground at Ile Aux Coudres in the St. Lawrence on July 20, 1940. Some 600 tons of coal were thrown overboard and at high tide the vessel was pulled free. The 260-foot-long member of the Paterson fleet had been built at Sunderland, England, in 1927 and after the Second World War joined Colonial Steamships as *Queenston*. The hull survives as a dock facing at Bob-Lo Island in the Detroit River. (Doug Mackie Collection)

Thorold had just left the Great Lakes and was carrying coal from Cardiff, Wales, to London when the 258-foot-long bulk carrier was attacked by the Luftwaffe. The vessel was machine gunned and bombed for ninety minutes, setting fires and causing heavy damage. Eleven on board were killed, three were injured and thirteen were rescued when the ship went down on August 22, 1940. (Earl D. Simzer Collection, courtesy George Ayoub)

A. E. Ames had come to Canada following construction in England during 1903. The 257-foot-long vessel returned to saltwater in 1917. It was owned by French interests and sailing as the *Ginette Laborgne* when it was lost. The ship hit a mine and sank in the Mediterranean west of Sardinia on September 12, 1940. (Alfred Sagon-King)

Trevisa was headed overseas with a load of timber when the ship was torpedoed by *U 124*. Small and therefore hindered more by strong winds, the ship had fallen behind its convoy, SC-7, and was the first to be picked off. Seven lives were lost when the ship went down 600 miles off the coast of Ireland on October 16, 1940. A total of twenty ships were sunk in that convoy during three nights of attacks. (Ernest R. Longman)

Sparta was working through a heavy gale and snow when it stranded on a reef near the beautiful Pictured Rocks off Munising, Michigan. The 400-foot-long bulk carrier hit on November 5, 1940 and was abandoned on November 11. The ship was salvaged the next spring but was too badly damaged to be repaired. Part of the hull became a drydock and part was used as a breakwall. (Taylor Photo, Collection of Peter Worden)

Anna C. Minch was a victim of the terrible Armistice Day Storm that swept Lake Michigan on November 11, 1940. The 400-foot ship disappeared with all hands off Pentwater, Michigan, while carrying screenings from Fort William to Chicago. Twenty-five sailors were lost aboard the 37-year-old Canadian bulk carrier. (Alfred King)

William B. Davock was built in 1907 and joined the Interlake Steamship Company in 1915. The 440-foot-long bulk carrier had loaded 7,240 tons of coal at Erie, Pennsylvania, and was bound for South Chicago when it disappeared on November 11, 1940, off Pentwater, Michigan. All thirty-two sailors on board perished. The hull was found resting upside down in 250 feet of water in 1972. (Great Lakes Graphics)

Novadoc was also lost near Pentwater on November 11, 1940. It was en route from Chicago to Port Alfred, Quebec. The ship ran aground in the vicious storm and broke its back. The crew huddled in their cabins for thirty-six hours before help arrived. Two cooks were swept overboard trying to get to the forward cabin. Eventually seventeen were saved from the 12-year-old, 259-foot-long member of the Paterson fleet but the vessel was a total loss. (Doug Mackie Collection)

The rail car ferry *City of Flint 32* hit bottom outside Ludington, Michigan, during the Armistice Day Storm and lost headway. The 381-foot, 6-inch vessel landed in shallow water and was scuttled to save it from breaking up. The vessel was refloated and required repairs to fifteen plates, the rudder and rudder post. It became the flat-deck river barge *Roanoke* in 1970. (Paul Michaels Collection)

Sinaloa, loaded with sand, stranded near Big Bay de Noc, Lake Michigan, on November 11-12, 1940, after losing its rudder. The crew were saved by local fishermen. The 441-foot-long self-unloader, built at West Bay City, Michigan in 1903, was refloated and repaired. It became *Stonefax* in 1960 and was scrapped at Santander, Spain, in 1971. (Peter Worden)

Four
1941 - 1950

Westcliffe Hall was built at South Bank, England, in 1928 and chartered to the British Ministry of War Transport in 1940. The 258-foot, 6-inch bulk carrier was bombed in enemy action in the North Sea on February 13, 1941 but was able to continue in service. The ship was returned to the Hall Corporation after the war and remained on the Great Lakes, becoming *Wheaton* in 1955. It was scrapped at Hamilton in 1965-66. (Al Sykes Collection)

The Norwegian freighter *Reinunga* came to the Great Lakes from 1926 to 1933. The 225-foot, 1-inch vessel, which had been built in 1902, had to spend the winter of 1932-33 at Dain City on the Welland Canal. The ship was sold and renamed *Kythera* in 1934. It became a war victim and was bombed and sunk by German aircraft at Suda Bay on May 16, 1941. (Ted Jones, courtesy Barry Andersen)

Kingston of Canada Steamship Lines became stuck on a shoal in the St. Lawrence on June 17, 1941. The 300-foot-long passenger ship stranded in fog west of Ogdensburg, New York, and was hit by lightning before it could be refloated with the aid of pontoons. The ship had been built at Toronto for the Lake Ontario passenger trade in 1901 and was scrapped at Hamilton in 1950. (John H. Bascom)

Rapids Prince spent two months aground in the Lachine Rapids west of Montreal. The vessel became stuck on July 6, 1941 and the 218 passengers had to be removed in motor boats. The 210-foot-long ship usually ran the St. Lawrence Rapids between Prescott and Montreal and returned upbound via the locks and canals. This carrier was retired late in 1949 and sold for scrapping at Stelco in Hamilton in 1951. (Gordon Crompton)

Collingdoc was one of several members of the Paterson fleet lost in the Second World War. The 261-foot vessel struck a mine off Southend, England, on July 13, 1941 and sank with the loss of two lives. The hull was refloated, taken north and resunk as a blockship off the Orkney Islands. The reinforced concrete pilothouse was all that could be seen among the shifting area sands in 2003. (Alfred King)

Mondoc stranded off the east coast of Trinidad on October 5, 1941 during its first trip on the Caribbean. It had gone south to help in the bauxite trade but was lost while travelling from Georgetown, British Guiana, to the British Virgin Islands. It is believed to have sunk after hitting Darien Rock. The crew took to the lifeboats and were rescued. (Earl D. Simzer Collection, courtesy George Ayoub)

Oakbay had been built in France as *Marinier* in 1919 and came to the Great Lakes in 1922. It was sold and renamed *Henry C. Daryaw* in 1935 and rebuilt for the coal trade. The 230-foot-long ship was requisitioned for coastal service but stranded in the Brockville Narrows during the delivery voyage on November 21, 1941. The freighter sank in deep water during a salvage attempt. (John H. Bascom)

Makaweli was damaged in the Japanese air attack of Pearl Harbor on December 7, 1941. The tanker had been built at Ashtabula, Ohio, as *Cowee* in 1919. It had to be towed to San Pedro, California, for repairs after the attack. The 261-foot-long vessel returned to the Great Lakes and operated for Lakeland Tankers from 1946 to 1966. *Makaweli* was scrapped in Italy in 1967. (Ted Jones, courtesy Barry Andersen)

Lake Gorin was built at Wyandotte, Michigan, and joined the United States Shipping Board in 1918. The 261-foot steamer was idle on the East Coast when purchased by the Ford Motor Company for scrap in the 1920s. *Lake Gorin* was towed back to the Great Lakes but repowered for further service instead of being broken up. The ship was resold to a Norwegian firm as *Nidardal* in 1938 and foundered on December 16, 1941. (Earl D. Simzer Collection, courtesy George Ayoub)

Lake Flambeau was built at Duluth in 1919 for the United States Shipping Board, but was completed too late for first world war duty. The 261-foot-long freighter operated on saltwater and was later renamed *James River* and then *Frances Salman*. It was attacked by *U 552* on January 18, 1942 off the coast of Newfoundland. The ship sank in eight minutes and twenty-eight lives were lost. (Alex Duncan)

George L. Torian was loaded with bauxite when it was torpedoed by *U 129* off the coast of British Guiana on February 22, 1942. The survivors clung to debris for twenty-four hours until rescued by an American vessel. The 261-foot freighter violently exploded when hit and it sank quickly. The ship had sailed on the Great Lakes for Eastern Steamships and the Upper Lakes and St. Lawrence Transportation Company. (Alfred King)

Lennox was another victim of *U 129*. It was one of seven ships sunk by this submarine in a two week period. *Lennox* was a 261-foot-long bulk carrier and dated from 1923. It was heading to Trinidad with bauxite when hit. This ship, which belonged to Canada Steamship Lines, did not explode and eighteen of the twenty men on board were saved following the attack on February 23, 1942. (Alfred King)

Robert W. Pomeroy was requisitioned by the British Ministry of War Transport in 1940 and went overseas for coastal service around the United Kingdom. The 262-foot-long bulk carrier was northbound in a convoy when it reportedly struck two mines on the port side of the ship. Although there were injuries, the crew survived, but the ship sank in the North Sea off Norfolk on April 1, 1942. (Earl D. Simzer Collection, courtesy George Ayoub)

Canadian Farmer cost $711,720 to build at Collingwood and the 261-foot freighter was launched into Georgian Bay on December 27, 1919. It went to the Atlantic the next year, was registered in France as *Wester* in 1934, and then served in the Far East becoming *Shinkuang* in 1935. Japanese surface forces attacked and sank the vessel in the Bay of Bengal on April 6, 1942. (Collingwood Museum)

Mont Louis was built for the Hall Corporation and launched at Middlesborough, England, on May 13, 1927. This 261-foot-long vessel left the Great Lakes and went to the Caribbean for the bauxite trade in the Second World War. The ship was torpedoed by *U 162* on May 8, 1942. Thirteen lives were lost when it sank. Eight crew survived and were picked up and delivered to Georgetown, British Guiana. (Earl D. Simzer Collection, courtesy George Ayoub)

Torondoc left St. Thomas, Virgin Islands, for Trinidad on May 18, 1942 and was never heard from again. German broadcasts claimed that the 260-foot-long bulk carrier was torpedoed by *U 69* on May 21. The vessel was believed to have gone down off Martinique and there were no survivors from the crew of nineteen. This 15-year-old member of the Paterson fleet was on the Caribbean for the bauxite trade. (Earl D. Simzer Collection, courtesy George Ayoub)

Troisdoc, another member of the Paterson fleet, was also lost on May 21, 1942. This ship was hit by torpedoes from *U 558* while forty miles west of Jamaica. The first one did not explode but the second did. The crew escaped to the lifeboats and were picked up after five hours adrift. The 14-year-old freighter was travelling in ballast from St. Thomas, Virgin Islands, to Georgetown, British Guiana. (Earl D. Simzer Collection, courtesy George Ayoub)

Fred W. Green had been built as *Craycroft* and launched at Ecorse, Michigan, on September 26, 1918. The 261-foot, 10-inch steamer left for coastal service but returned to the Great Lakes in 1927 for the sand, stone and coal trades. The ship was back on the Atlantic in the Second World War and was en route from New York to Sierra Leone with trucks, ammonia and nitric acid when it was attacked and sunk by *U 506* on May 30, 1942. Five sailors, including the captain, were lost. (Milwaukee Public Library)

The *Eugene J. Buffington* struck Boulder Reef, Lake Michigan, on June 23, 1942. It spent twenty-five days aground and its back broke in two places. The hull was salvaged and carefully towed to Chicago for repairs. The 601-foot, 1-inch bulk carrier of the Pittsburgh Steamship fleet would likely have been scrapped were it not for the demands of the Second World War. The ship sailed many more years but was broken up in Spain during 1980-81. (Paul Michaels Collection)

Coalhaven sank at Thorold, Ontario, in July 1942 after an unloading mishap. The boom had swung away from the dock tilting the ship to starboard and water rushed into the engine room through an open door. The 258-foot-long self-unloader belonged to Canada Steamship Lines from 1928 to 1962 and then sailed for Bayswater Shipping as *Bayfair* until scrapped in 1969-70. (Alfred King)

The *Donald Stewart* was in convoy carrying 45-gallon drums of aviation fuel plus bulk cement for building runways at the Goose Bay Air Force Base when it was torpedoed by *U 517*. The gasoline ignited when the first torpedo hit and the 261-foot ship sank in seven minutes near the Strait of Belle Isle. Three sailors in the engine room were lost when the vessel went down on September 3, 1942. (Earl D. Simzer Collection, courtesy George Ayoub)

Steel Vendor was used to carry steel products and often travelled between the Great Lakes and the east coast. The 258-foot, 3-inch vessel had a load of steel billets that shifted in a Lake Superior storm while east of Keweenaw Point on September 3, 1942. Water poured in but the crew was able to get off the ship, with the last man leaving six minutes before the vessel sank. (Earl D. Simzer Collection, courtesy George Ayoub)

Canatco was built for the Canadian government and launched at Collingwood as *Canadian Gunner* on October 14, 1919. The 261-foot-long vessel operated between Canada and the West Indies in the sugar trade but returned to the Great Lakes as *Canatco* in 1927. It was wrecked at Hamilton Inlet, Labrador, in October 1942 (one source gives the date as October 2 and another as October 24). (Great Lakes Graphics)

Waterton joined the Bowater Steamship Company in May 1941 after thirteen years on the Great Lakes. The 258-foot-long vessel operated in and around Newfoundland until it was lost by enemy action on October 11, 1942. The ship, which was carrying newsprint, went down in eight minutes after it was attacked by *U 106*. All on board were rescued. (Earl D. Simzer Collection, courtesy George Ayoub)

Judge Hart stranded on Fitzsimmons Rock, Ashburton Bay, Lake Superior, on November 27, 1942 but slid off the ledge when the engine stopped. The 261-foot, 19-year-old freighter of the Upper Lakes and St. Lawrence Transportation Company fleet was loaded with grain for Toronto. The hull drifted and sank but all twenty-one crew on board were rescued. (Earl D. Simzer Collection, courtesy George Ayoub)

Gotham 85, a steel tank barge, was renamed *Cleveco* in 1941. The 250-foot vessel had several names after it was built for Standard Oil in 1913. *Cleveco* was carrying crude oil and had gone to anchor when it was lost with all hands off Euclid Beach, Ohio, on December 3, 1942. A total of thirty-two lives, including fourteen crew on the towing tug *Admiral* which also sank, and eighteen on the barge, were lost. (Alfred King)

Hamildoc was working in the Caribbean bauxite trade when it foundered on January 1, 1943. The ship had gone to anchor while travelling from British Guiana to Trinidad but broke in two during a three-day gale. The 259-foot-long vessel had been built at Sunderland, England, in 1927 and sailed on the Great Lakes as part of the Paterson fleet before going south. All on board were saved. (Ted Jones, courtesy Barry Andersen)

The Norwegian freighter *Listo* had been built by the Port Arthur Shipbuilding Company and completed as *War Osiris* in July 1918. The 2,264 gross ton vessel had been owned by The Shipping Controller of Great Britain before it became *Colmar* in 1920 and *Listo* in 1929. It struck a mine and sank near Spodsbjerg, Denmark, on February 16, 1943. (Shipsearch Marine)

The 376-foot *Prindoc* left Fort William on May 31, 1943 with 211,527 bushels of wheat on board. A collision the next day in heavy fog off Passage Island, Lake Superior, also involved the freighter *Battleford*. *Prindoc*, part of the N.M. Paterson fleet, had no collision bulkhead and sank. The crew of twenty-two sailors, including the master who had survived the loss of the *Novadoc*, (p. 85) were rescued. (Kenneth E. Smith)

Battleford had only recently returned to service after it was rebuilt for the package freight trade in 1939. It was carrying pig iron, steel pipe and general packaged freight when it sank *Prindoc* in the June 1, 1943, collision. The 261-foot-long *Battleford* left the Great Lakes in 1967 and operated around the Bahamas as *Real Gold* before it was laid up in 1971. The ship was scrapped at Tampico, Mexico, in 1974. (Al Sykes Collection)

Orsa was built at Superior, Wisconsin, and completed in May 1943 for the United States Maritime Commission as the *William Brewster*. It loaded wheat for England but sank while leaving the Great Lakes. A collision with the *W. D. Calverley Jr.* off Algonac, Michigan, on June 15, 1943 led to a hasty decision to beach the vessel which then rolled on its side. The freighter was not refloated until November 1943 and after repairs operated on saltwater. It was renamed *Orsa* in 1949 and was scrapped at India as *Ray Mayabundar* in June 1967. (World Ship Society)

George M. Humphrey was the first ship of over 600 feet to be lost on the Great Lakes. The ore-laden bulk carrier went down off Old Point Mackinac Light on June 15, 1943, after a collision with the *D. M. Clemson*. A massive salvage effort was successful on September 15, 1944 and the ship was rebuilt at Sturgeon Bay, Wisconsin. The vessel, later the *Consumers Power*, had been constructed in 1927. It arrived at Kaohsiung, Taiwan, on October 2, 1988 to be broken up. (Great Lakes Graphics)

Coastal Cliff was named *Bruce Hudson* when it caught fire at South Chicago while loading 11,000 barrels of high octane gasoline on July 26, 1943. The captain, his son and two members of the crew were killed. This tanker had been built as a barge in 1935 and was powered in 1938-39. It was renamed *Coastal Cliff* in 1952 and was scrapped at Cartagena, Colombia, as *Witcroix* about 1983. (Al Sykes Collection)

Riverton stranded on Lottie Wolf Shoal, Georgian Bay, in November 1943. The 470-foot-long bulk carrier had previously been wrecked as *L.C. Waldo* in Lake Superior on November 8, 1913, but was rebuilt after each accident. The 1896-vintage vessel was refloated on November 30, 1943 and resumed trading as *Mohawk Deer*. It sank for the third and final time in the Gulf of Genoa, on November 6, 1967 en route to scrapping in Italy. (Alfred King)

Santa Eulalia made four trips to the Great Lakes in 1933 after it was built at Toledo, Ohio, as *Lake Finney* in 1920. The 258-foot vessel was sold to an Italian firm as *Polecevera* in 1938 and was seized by the Germans in 1943. *H.M.S. Torbay*, a British submarine, torpedoed and sank the former laker on November 27, 1943. (Earl D. Simzer Collection, courtesy George Ayoub)

Sarnian was the first vessel purchased by what is now Upper Lakes Shipping. The 344-foot bulk carrier stranded on Pointe Isabelle Reef, Lake Superior, carrying 162,489 bushels of barley on December 9, 1943. The ship was refloated on June 24, 1944 and laid up. It had been built as *Chili* in 1895, and was scrapped at Indiana Harbor, Indiana, in 1947. (Laurence Scott, courtesy Al Sykes)

James H. Reed was lost in a collision when thick fog blanketed Lake Erie on April 27, 1944. The accident occurred at 0530 hours while the ship was north of Conneaut, Ohio. Twelve sailors were lost when the 468-foot-long ore carrier sank in 66 feet of water. Another twenty-four on board were picked up by the *Ashcroft*, the other ship involved in the collision. Later the hull of the *James H. Reed* had to be dynamited, as its location was a hazard to navigation. (Great Lakes Graphics)

Frank E. Vigor was making its way downbound through the foggy Pelee Island passage when it was lost. The 432-foot-long crane ship, laden with sulphur, collided with the *Philip Minch* at 0850 hours on April 27, 1944 and the freighter sank in seventy-five feet of water. All thirty-two sailors on the 48-year-old vessel were rescued. (Milwaukee Public Library)

The *Philip Minch* was travelling in ballast when it sank the *Frank E. Vigor* on April 27, 1944. The 500-foot-long bulk carrier served the Kinsman Transit Company from 1905 to 1968 and was used to haul iron, coal or grain. It was sold for scrap and towed to Santander, Spain, in September 1969 to be broken up. (Paul Michaels Collection)

Albert C. Field was providing support for the invasion of Normandy when it was sunk in the English Channel by a torpedo and air attack on June 18, 1944. The vessel was transporting 2,500 tons of munitions and 130 bags of U.S. Mail to France when it was hit. The hull broke in two and sank within three minutes. Four sailors on board the 261-foot-long freighter were lost. (Earl D. Simzer Collection, courtesy George Ayoub)

Erling Lindoe had been built in 1917 and came to the Great Lakes in 1933 and 1934. The 236-foot, 9-inch Norwegian freighter was lost after striking a mine in the Kattegat Strait between Denmark and Sweden on August 11, 1944. The ship sank and thirteen members of the crew were lost. (Clyde Sandelin, courtesy Dan McCormick)

The 16-year-old *Livingston* was rebuilt for war service during the Second World War. A deck cabin was added to house a gun crew after the ship left the Great Lakes for service to and from Newfoundland. The 258-foot-long vessel was torpedoed and sunk by *U 541* on September 3, 1944 while travelling about eighty miles east of Cape Breton Island. Fourteen lives, including one of the gun crew, were lost while an equal number were rescued. (Earl D. Simzer Collection, courtesy George Ayoub)

Westmount came to the Great Lakes in 1903 as a replacement for the ill-fated *Bannockburn*. The 255-foot-long freighter was purchased by German interests in 1937 and was renamed for the sixth time, as *Ludolf Oldendorff*. To the Allies of the Second World War it had thus become an enemy ship and was sunk by British aircraft at Egersund, Norway, on October 9, 1944. (Craig Workman Collection)

The Second World War was almost over when the *Nipiwan Park* was torpedoed in the Atlantic Ocean on January 4, 1945. Two crewmen were killed when the forward end was blown away but amazingly the ship did not sink. The 259-foot-long tanker was towed to Pictou, Nova Scotia and fitted with a new 150-foot bow. The ship had been built at Collingwood in 1944 and became *Irvinglake* in 1952. (Ted Jones, courtesy Barry Andersen)

The *George T. Davie* was built at Lauzon, Quebec, in 1898. The 177-foot, 6-inch barge was used to carry grain and later operated across Lake Ontario hauling coal from Oswego, New York, to ports in Ontario. It had 1,100 tons of coal on board when water began to pour in through the forward hatch causing the vessel to sink on April 18, 1945. It went down in eighty-five feet of water off Nine Mile Point. (Clyde Sandelin, courtesy Dan McCormick)

The Greek freighter *Eftychia* made one trip to the Great Lakes in 1961. The 436-foot-long cargo carrier was launched at Burntisland, U.K., on August 2, 1943 and first sailed as *Riverton*. It was torpedoed by *U 1023* off the southwest coast of England, on April 23, 1945 and three lives were lost. The ship was rebuilt and lasted until it was scrapped as *Boaz Esperanza* at Kaohsiung, Taiwan, in 1969. (Paul Michaels Collection)

Moyra was built at Sunderland, England, in 1931 and often visited the Great Lakes for the Warren Line. The ship was damaged by a fire twenty miles east of Quebec City on May 11-13, 1945 and had to be beached off Ile d'Orleans. The vessel was repaired and returned to the Great Lakes as the Norwegian *Heika*. Renamed *Marisco* in 1956, it sank off the coast of Greece on October 20, 1959. (Earl D. Simzer Collection, courtesy George Ayoub)

Hamonic was built like an ocean liner and was considered a very safe and seaworthy vessel. It was constructed at Collingwood Shipyards and launched as their Hull 22 on November 26, 1908. The 365-foot-long passenger and freight carrier was popular with the travelling public and operated a weekly schedule between Point Edward, the Canadian Lakehead and Duluth. (Ken Lowes)

Hamonic was moored beside the Point Edward freight shed when the structure caught fire on July 17, 1945. The flames ignited the wooden deck of the ship but the captain calmly steered his burning vessel out of harm's way. This enabled all on board to evacuate safely. *Hamonic* was a total loss and the remains of the hull were taken to Hamilton and broken up in 1946. (Collingwood Museum)

Outarde was tied up at the Consul-Hall Dock at Clayton, New York, when a wild storm repeatedly pounded the hull against the dock. Water poured in through an opening and the ship sank with an awkward list on November 30, 1945. The vessel was not successfully refloated until April 18, 1946, after a previous attempt had failed. (Ken Lowes)

Outarde had come to Canada as *Brulin* in 1924 and was renamed when it joined the Quebec and Ontario Transportation Company in 1939. The 261-foot-long vessel returned to service in June 1946 and was lost as the *James J. Buckler* near the mouth of the Saguenay River on June 16, 1960. (Ted Jones, courtesy Barry Andersen)

Georgian was one of several names for this once familiar Great Lakes trader. It is perhaps most famous for being the first upbound transit when the Fourth Welland Canal opened on April 21, 1930. The 258-foot-long freighter had several accidents on the Great Lakes but was lost in the Gulf of Mexico as *Badger State* after striking a sunken hulk on January 14, 1946. (Alfred King)

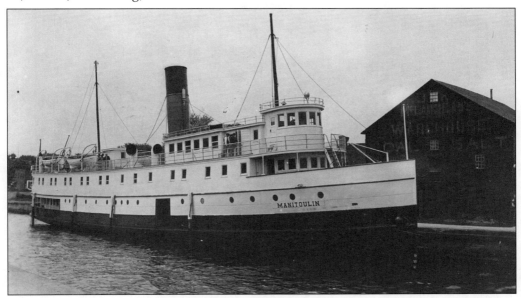

Manitoulin dated from 1889 and had been built at Glasgow, Scotland, for Lake Ontario service as *Modjeska*. It was rebuilt and renamed in 1927. The ship was used to carry passengers and freight between Owen Sound and other Georgian Bay ports to Sault Ste. Marie. On May 20, 1946 *Manitoulin* ran aground on Clapperton Island and was released the next day. It was retired in 1949 and scrapped at St. Catharines in 1951-52. (James Studio)

Teakbay was lit up by the spotlight of a Nazi U-boat on the Gulf of St. Lawrence during the Second World War. But, after following the 259-foot-long pulpwood carrier, the enemy had decided not to use up a torpedo. *Teakbay* later ran aground on Featherbed Shoal off Carleton Island in the St. Lawrence on July 29, 1946. It was refloated and continued to sail until the end of 1962. The 35-year-old freighter was broken up for scrap at Hamilton in 1964. (Daniel C. McCormick)

Hai Lin began working on the Great Lakes in 1912 as the *Lucius W. Robinson*. The 257-foot-long bulk carrier went to the Atlantic for both world wars and was sold to the Wah Shang Steamship Company in 1946. Renamed *Hai Lin*, it left Montreal for the Far East and encountered three Pacific typhoons en route, including one while anchored at Saipan, Philippines, on September 21, 1946. The 15,528-mile journey to Shanghai, China, took 122 days. (R. Larouche, courtesy Daniel C. McCormick)

Kindersley was built at Glasgow, Scotland, in 1909 and sailed as *A. E. McKinstry* until 1927. The 258-foot-long steamship left Canada for war duty in 1940 and was bombed by German aircraft on August 16, 1941. The damage was repaired and *Kindersley* served until peace returned. After the war, the hull was filled with 2,074 tons of surplus munitions and scuttled in the Atlantic on October 1, 1946. (George Ayoub)

On March 12, 1947, *Exanthia* struck a second-world-war mine on the Mediterranean near the island of Elba. The ship flooded and was initially abandoned. Reboarded, it was taken in tow and beached. *Exanthia* was unloaded, refloated and taken to New York for repairs. The 420-foot-long vessel made nine trips to the Great Lakes from 1959 to 1961 and was scrapped at Brownsville, Texas, in 1975. (Jon O'Leary, courtesy Jim Bartke)

Emperor (see also p. 72) ran aground in calm but foggy weather, hitting the Canoe Rocks off Isle Royale on June 4, 1947. One lifeboat got away but the other one was sucked under. The ore-laden, 525-foot-long bulk carrier slid back into the deep waters of Lake Superior and was a total loss. Twelve sailors died in the mishap. (Scott McWilliam)

Translake was upbound with a cargo of crude oil when it unexpectedly turned broadside in the channel near Iroquois, Ontario. The downbound *Milverton* slammed into the tanker on September 24, 1947, causing crude oil to leak into the river and the *Translake* to go aground. The 228-foot, 6-inch vessel had been built in France in 1921 and was repaired. It eventually worked as a barge and was scrapped at Louiseville, Quebec, about 1980. (Daniel C. McCormick)

Milverton erupted in flames when its fuel lines ruptured in the collision with the *Translake* on September 24, 1947. The ship drifted downstream and grounded at the head of Rapide Plat. The coal-laden vessel burned for two days and eleven lives were lost. *Milverton* was eventually refloated, brought to Port Weller Dry Docks for repairs and returned to service. (Ken Lowes)

Clary Foran, which burned as the *Milverton*, resumed trading in 1949 for the Sarnia Steamship Company. The 259-foot-long freighter, built in Glasgow, Scotland, in 1929, continued to work in the bulk trades through the old canals. It was sold and renamed *Ferndale* in 1959 and scrapped by Stelco at Hamilton in 1963. (Ken Lowes)

William C. Warren was caught by a fall gale and driven aground near Presque Isle Point, Lake Huron, on November 7, 1947. A quick salvage was impossible and the ship was stuck for the winter although the cargo of grain was blown ashore through a pipeline. The vessel was refloated the following spring and taken to Collingwood for repairs. (Alan Mann)

William C. Warren returned to work for Beaconsfield Steamships only to go aground near Port Colborne on November 1, 1948, during its first trip for the new owner. The 261-foot-long bulk carrier had been built for the Eastern Steamship Company at Old Kirkpatrick, Scotland, in 1925 and was scrapped at Montreal in 1964-65. (Jay Bascom)

Harry L. Findlay was sailing as *Matthew Andrews* when it grounded at Corsica Shoal, Lake Huron, in the Great Storm of November 1913. The 552-foot-long freighter was renamed in 1933. It was in collision with the Canadian tanker *John Irwin* in the St. Clair River, near Recors Point, on April 24, 1948. Both ships were repaired. The *Harry L. Findlay* became *Paul L. Tietjen* in 1965 and was scrapped at Ashtabula, Ohio, in 1979, at the age of 72. (Paul Michaels Collection)

Crete had a head-on collision in fog near Apostle Island, Lake Superior, on June 23, 1948. The bow was pushed back twenty feet when it struck the *J. P. Morgan Jr.* The 500-foot-long *Crete* went to Superior, Wisconsin, for repairs. This member of the Interlake Steamship Company fleet had been launched on September 7, 1907 and was scrapped at Savona, Italy, after a long tow, in 1962. (Paul Sherlock)

The cabin of the *J. P. Morgan Jr.* was crushed in the collision with the *Crete* on June 23, 1948. Two sailors were killed in their rooms and it is amazing neither freighter sank. The 601-foot-long *J. P. Morgan Jr.* had been built at Lorain, Ohio, in 1910 and worked for United States Steel. It last sailed in 1974 and was scrapped at Aviles, Spain, in 1980-81. (Paul Michaels Collection)

Grainmotor was launched in August 1929 as the first of a new breed of diesel powered bulk carriers designed for the old St. Lawrence Canals. Because of the Depression, it was also the last to be built. The 257-foot-long freighter lost power in the Welland Canal on July 30, 1948 and dropped anchor. The ship went out of control and bounced off both banks, turning completely around before coming to a stop. The vessel worked for Canada Steamship Lines until 1964 and then operated on saltwater. (Daniel C. McCormick)

Harry T. Ewig was launched at Chicago on February 1, 1902 and had several names and owners. The 366-foot-long steamship received deck cranes in 1939 and these were used for loading and unloading a variety of cargoes. The vessel received about $40,000 in damage when it went aground off Point Abino, Lake Erie on October 24, 1948. The hull was refloated but was cut in two to make a pair of barges in 1964. (Paul Michaels Collection)

The *John J. Boland* collided with the *Frank Armstrong* near Southeast Shoal, Lake Erie, on November 2, 1948. The accident resulted in the loss of one life and $352,864 in damage to the bow and forward cabins. The 500-foot-long freighter sailed under four different names for the American Steamship Company and was scrapped as *Peavey Pioneer* of the Kinsman fleet at Duluth in 1968-69. (Paul Michaels Collection)

Fort Willdoc was built in 1900 as *John J. Albright*. It was renamed *Regulus* in 1916 and *Fort Willdoc* in 1926. The 436-foot-long bulk carrier lost its rudder while crossing Lake Superior in 1941 and received $70,000 in damage in a collision with the *James E. McAlpine* on April 6, 1949. The accident occurred above Whitefish Point, Lake Superior. This member of the Paterson fleet was repaired and operated until late 1964. (Ted Jones, courtesy Barry Andersen)

James E. McAlpine received bow damage in the April 6, 1949, collision with the *Fort Willdoc*. The 452-foot-long bulk carrier, part of the Brown Steamship Company fleet, had been built as the *William H. Truesdale* in 1908 and was towed to Genoa, Italy, for scrapping in 1965. (Jay Bascom)

The Second World War Flower class corvette HMCS *Battleford* was built at Collingwood in 1941. It was involved in convoy duty during the Second World War and saw considerable action, including assistance in the destruction of *U 356*. The ship was sold to the Venezuelan Navy and renamed *Liberdad* in 1946, but was wrecked on April 12, 1949. (Ken Macpherson Collection)

The second *New York News* hit a shoal at the east entrance to Little Current, Ontario, on July 8, 1949. The accident was blamed on low water levels and a misplaced channel marker. The 261-foot-long bulk carrier was inbound with coal and 800 tons had to be removed before the ship could float free. The vessel had survived a close call on the Gulf of St. Lawrence during the Second World War when the freighter ahead was sunk by a torpedo. (Ken Lowes)

Northumberland was built at Newcastle, England, in 1891 and initially operated between Pictou, Nova Scotia, and Charlottetown, Prince Edward Island. The 232-foot-long passenger steamer came to the Great Lakes in 1920 and sailed with passengers and freight between Toronto and Port Dalhousie. The vessel could carry 1050 passengers and burned 4.4 tons of coal in the two-hour and ten-minute trip across the western end of Lake Ontario. (Jay Bascom)

Northumberland was fitting out for the new season when it caught fire at the dock in Port Dalhousie on June 2, 1949. The blaze apparently began in a washroom and spread quickly throughout the ship, fueled by the freshly painted woodwork. The firemen could not save the vessel. All on board got off safely but *Northumberland* was a total loss and the remains were broken up at Port Weller Dry Docks. (*St. Catharines Standard*)

Noronic was launched at Port Arthur, Ontario, on June 2, 1913 and was considered the most palatial steamer on the Great Lakes at the time. The 385-foot-long vessel served Canada Steamship Lines on a weekly schedule and carried passengers and freight between Detroit, Sarnia, Sault Ste. Marie and the Canadian Lakehead. Pre and post season cruises took *Noronic* to Georgian Bay and Lake Ontario ports. (Roger Chapman Collection)

Noronic was at Toronto on a post season voyage to the Thousand Islands when fire broke out in a linen closet on September 17, 1949. The blaze tore through the ship and 118 lost their lives. The beautiful vessel was totally destroyed in the worst shipping loss in Lake Ontario history. *Noronic* sank at the dock but was pumped out, towed to Hamilton and scrapped. (Al Sykes Collection)

City of Cleveland III burned prior to completion in 1907 and was rebuilt, complete with luxurious accommodations, for the Detroit and Cleveland Navigation Company. The 402-foot-long passenger liner was struck by the *Ravnefjell* on foggy lake Huron during a Chamber of Commerce cruise. Five lives were lost in the June 25, 1950 accident and the ship was laid up and not repaired. The remains of the hull were broken up at Buffalo. (Dave Glick Collection)

The Norwegian freighter *Ravnefjell*, a regular traveller to the Great Lakes, struck the *City of Cleveland III* amidships in the June 25, 1950 collision on Lake Huron. The 250-foot, 9-inch ocean visitor was repaired and continued service to our shores even after becoming *Ringstein* in 1955. The ship, then known as *Altair*, stranded near Achowa Point, Ghana, on September 11, 1966 and was a total loss. (Hubert Hall)

John M. McKerchey was a small, 161-foot-long self-unloader that dated from 1906. It was often used in the coal trade but also had the ability to draw sand from the lake bottom for delivery to shore. The ship got caught in a Lake Erie storm off Lorain, Ohio, where it capsized and sank on October 16, 1950. The captain was the only casualty. (Great Lakes Graphics)

Mapleton was built at Sunderland, England, in 1909 and worked on the Great Lakes before returning to the Atlantic during the Second World War. The 258-foot-long vessel was sold in 1948 and operated as *Eastern Med* under the flag of Cyprus. The ship was being loaded with oil drums at Port Suez, Egypt, on November 22, 1950 when a fire broke out and destroyed the freighter. The remains were scrapped. (Alfred King)

The cargo of steel and package freight aboard the *Weyburn* shifted in a Lake Ontario storm on November 25, 1950. The 261-foot-long steamship took a list to port and was in danger of sinking. Two other vessels stood by and one was able to tow *Weyburn* to the safety of Toronto Harbour. The ship served Canada Steamship Lines from 1927 until entering saltwater service in 1963. It was scrapped in Pakistan in 1966. (John H. Bascom)

On December 18, 1950, *Sachem* left Buffalo for Dunkirk, New York, and was swamped by a Lake Erie storm. The 43-year-old, 71-foot, 8-inch tug disappeared, taking the lives of twelve sailors. After searchers spotted an oil slick, the hull was located upright on the bottom and refloated on October 22, 1951. After repairs, *Sachem* returned to service and has been known as *Derek E.* since 1990. (SG)